It's Easy To Play Clayderman 2.

Wise Publications
London/New York/Sydney

Exclusive Distributors:
Music Sales Limited
8/9 Frith Street, London, W1V 5TZ, England.
Music Sales Pty. Limited
120 Rothschild Avenue, Rosebery, NSW 2018, Australia.

This book © Copyright 1987 by
Wise Publications
ISBN 0.7119.1139.8
Order No. AM 65921

Art direction by Mike Bell.
Cover illustration by Mark Thomas.
Compiled and arranged by Frank Booth.

Music Sales complete catalogue lists thousands of
titles and is free from your local music book shop,
or direct from Music Sales Limited.
Please send £1.75 Cheque/Postal Order for postage to
Music Sales Limited, 8/9 Frith Street, London W1V 5TZ

Unauthorised reproduction of any part of this publication by
any means including photocopying is an infringement of copyright.

Printed in England by
Caligraving Limited, Thetford, Norfolk.

Couleur Tendresse

Composed by Paul de Senneville & Olivier Toussaint

© Copyright 1982 Delphine Editions for the World.
Zomba Music Publishers Limited, 165-167 Willesden High Road, London NW10 for the UK & Eire.
All Rights Reserved. International Copyright Secured.

Lady 'Di'

Composed by Paul de Senneville & Jean Baudlot
Lyric by Paul de Senneville

© Copyright 1981 Delphine Editions for the World.
Zomba Music Publishers Limited, 165-167 Willesden High Road, London NW10 for the UK & Eire.
All Rights Reserved. International Copyright Secured.

L'Heure Bleue

Composed by Olivier Toussaint

© Copyright 1980 Tremplin/Delphine Editions for the World.
Zomba Music Publishers Limited, 165-167 Willesden High Road, London NW10 for the UK & Eire.
All Rights Reserved. International Copyright Secured.

Concerto Des Etoiles

Composed by Olivier Toussaint

© Copyright 1983 Delphine Editions for the World.
Zomba Music Publishers Limited, 165-167 Willesden High Road, London NW10 for the UK & Eire.
All Rights Reserved. International Copyright Secured.

Coda

La Fiancée Imaginaire

Composed by Paul Senneville

© Copyright 1982 Delphine Editions for the World.
Zomba Music Publishers Limited, 165-167 Willesden High Road, London NW10 for the UK & Eire.
All Rights Reserved. International Copyright Secured.

Histoire D'Un Rêve

Composed by Paul de Senneville

© Copyright 1980 Tremplin/Delphine Editions for the World.
Zomba Music Publishers Limited, 165-167 Willesden High Road, London NW 10 for the UK & Eire.
All Rights Reserved. International Copyright Secured.

Les Derniers Jours D'Anastasia

Composed by Paul de Senneville & Jean Baudlot
Lyric by Paul de Senneville

© Copyright 1981 Delphine Editions for the World.
Zomba Music Publishers Limited, 165-167 Willesden High Road, London NW10 for the UK & Eire.
All Rights Reserved. International Copyright Secured.

Serenade

Originally Composed by Franz Schubert
Arranged by Olivier Toussaint & Gerard Salesses

© Copyright 1982 Delphine Editions for the World.
Zomba Music Publishers Limited, 165-167 Willesden High Road, London NW10 for the UK & Eire.
All Rights Reserved. International Copyright Secured.

Feelings (Dime)

Spanish Lyrics by Thomas Fundora
Music & English Words by Morris Albert

© Copyright 1974, 1975 Editora Augusta Ltda, Brazil.
For the whole World except the American Continent: International Melodies Geneve, Switzerland.
Assigned for the territory of the United Kingdom & Eire to Bucks Music Ltd, 1a Farm Place, London, W8.
All Rights Reserved. International Copyright Secured.

Nostalgy

Composed by Olivier Toussaint

© Copyright 1979 Delphine Editions/Radio Music France for the World.
Zomba Music Publishers Limited, 165-167 Willesden High Road, London NW10 for the UK & Eire.
All Rights Reserved. International Copyright Secured.

I Have A Dream

Words & Music by Benny Andersson & Bjorn Ulvaeus

© Copyright 1979 for the World by Union Songs AB, Stockholm, Sweden.
Bocu Music Limited, 1 Wyndham Yard, Wyndham Place, London W1 for Great Britain & Eire.
All Rights Reserved. International Copyright Secured.

Guantanamera

Words by Jose Marti
Music Adaption by Hector Angulo & Peter Seeger

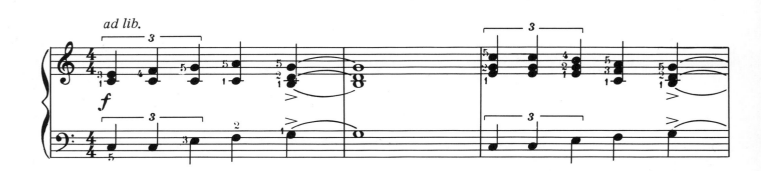

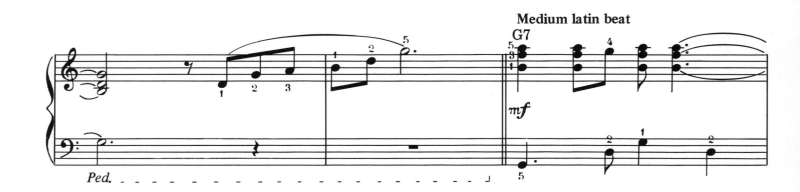

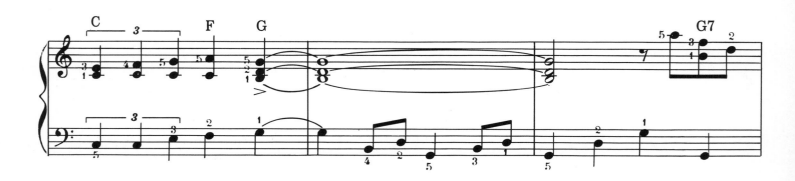

© Copyright 1963 & 1965 by Fall River Music Incorporation. New York, USA.
All rights for the British Commonwealth of Nations (excluding Canada and Australasia) and
the Republic of Eire controlled by Harmony Music Limited, 19-20 Poland Street, London W1.
All Rights Reserved. International Copyright Secured.

Reveries

Originally Composed by Robert Schumann
Arranged by Olivier Toussaint & Gerard Salesses

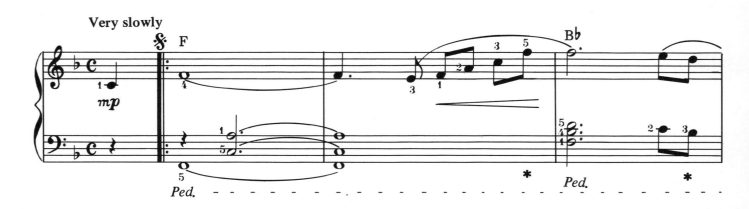

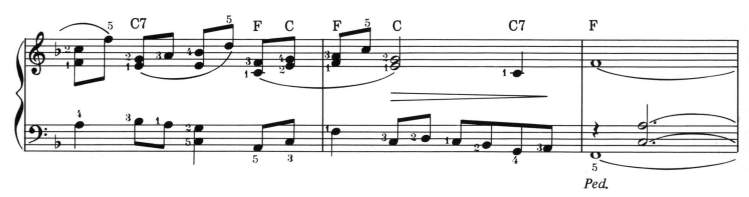

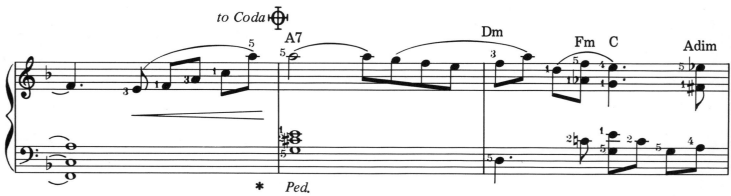

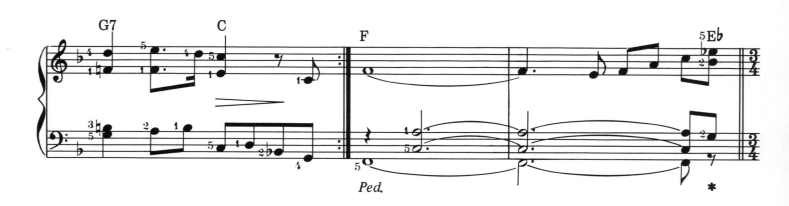

© Copyright 1982 Delphine Editions for the World.
Zomba Music Publishers Limited, 165-167 Willesden High Road, London NW10 for the UK & Eire.
All Rights Reserved. International Copyright Secured.

Les Roses De Sable

Composed by Paul de Senneville & Jean Baudlot

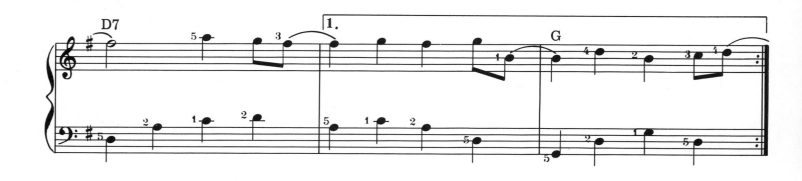

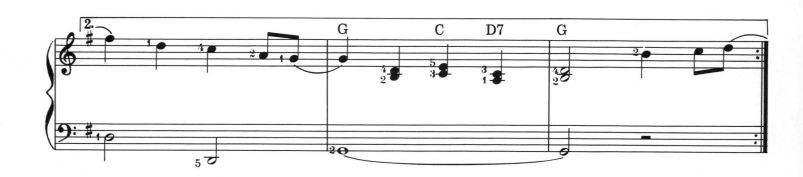

© Copyright 1982 Delphine Editions for the World.
Zomba Music Publishers Limited, 165-167 Willesden High Road, London NW10 for the UK & Eire.
All Rights Reserved. International Copyright Secured.

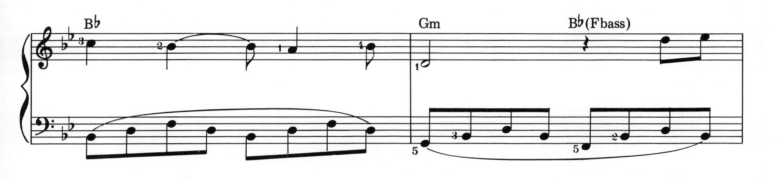

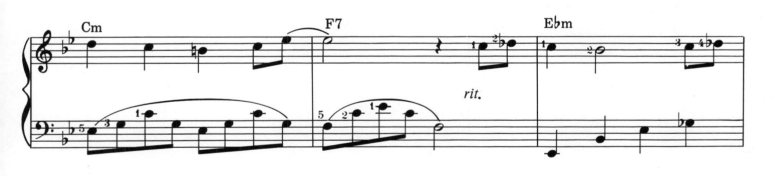

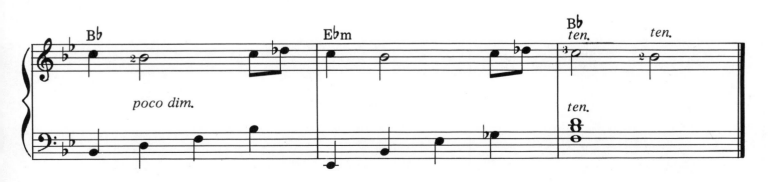

Checklist of important piano books

The books below are available from your local music shop
who will order them for you if not in stock.
If there is no music shop near you, you may order direct from
Music Sales Limited (Dept. M), 8/9 Frith Street, London, W1V 5TZ
Please always include £1 to cover post/packing costs.

A Start At The Piano
AM 40650

**Alison Bell's Graded
For Piano Pieces
Book 1: Very Easy**
AM 30297

**Book 5: Upper
Intermediate**
AM 30339

**Anthology Of Piano
Music Volume 1:
Baroque**
AM 10968

Volume 3: Romantic
AM 10984

**Barrelhouse And Boogie
Piano**
OK 64659

**Big Note Piano
Book 1**
AM 28226

**Bud Powell: Jazz
Masters Series**
AM 23219

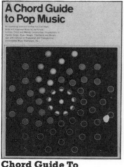
**Chord Guide To
Pop Music**
AM 10596

**The Classic Piano
Repertoire Bach**
EW 50023

Chopin
EW 50015

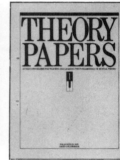
**Promenade Theory
Papers Book 1**
PB 40583

**Classics To Moderns
Book 1**
YK 20014

**Classics To Moderns
Sonatas & Sonatinas**
YK 20204

Themes & Variations
YK 20196

**More Classics To
Moderns Book 1**
YK 20121

**Dave Brubeck: Jazz
Masters Series**
AM 21189

**Easy Classical Piano
Duets**
AM 31949

**The Complete Piano
Player By Kenneth
Baker Book 1**
AM 34828

Book 2
AM 34836

Book 3
AM 34844

Book 4
AM 34851

Book 5
AM 34869

Style Book
AM 35338